HIGH
SIERRA
HIKING
GUIDE

MT. WHITNEY

D0092210

- trails
- trees
- history
- geology
- campsites
- wildflowers
- animals
- ecology
- fishing

Thomas Winnett

and including an updated USGS
topographic map of the area

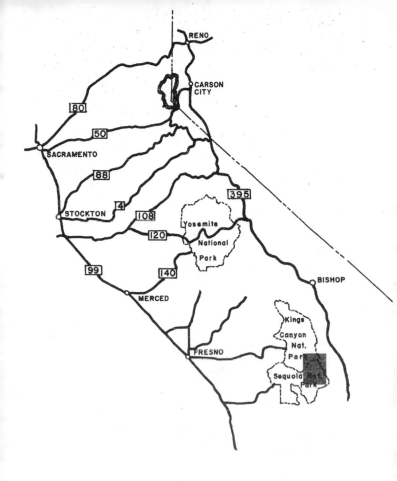

Location of the MT. WHITNEY quadrangle

High Sierra
Hiking Guide

Mt. Whitney

by Thomas Winnett

Drawings by Lucille Winnett

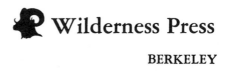 Wilderness Press

BERKELEY

Library of Congress Card Catalog Number 77-77224

International Standard Book Number 911824-62-6

Manufactured in the United States

Published by Wilderness Press
            2440 Bancroft Way
            Berkeley, CA 94704
            (415) 843-8080

Write for free catalog

Acknowledgments

For this second edition of Mt. Whitney, much had to be changed and updated. Fortunately, I was able to cover much of the quadrangle again myself, but I was even more fortunate to have the input of high-country lovers who can never stay away from this favorite quadrangle for long. For this input let me express deep appreciation to Alan Bradley, Don Denison, Don Harkin, Bill and Vicky Hoover, Bob Maynard, Gordon Peterson, Phil Pister, David Poast, Edwin Rockwell, John Allen Ryan, Peter Schuft, Helen Sharsmith, Robert L. Simpson, Jim Skillin and Andrew Smatko. My son Jason provided carrying power and moral support from Whitney Portal to Vidette Meadow (and beyond). Finally, my wife Lucille struggled to make the plants and animals in this book look the way I thought they ought to look.

—Thomas Winnett
Berkeley, Cal.
December 1977

PHOTO CREDITS

Introduction

The HIGH SIERRA HIKING GUIDES by the editors of Wilderness Press are the first *complete* guides to the famous High Sierra. Each guide covers one 15-minute U.S.G.S. topographic quadrangle, which is an area about 13 miles east-west by 17 miles north-south. The inside front cover shows the location of the quadrangle covered by this guide.

There is a great and increasing demand for literature about America's favorite wilderness, John Muir's "Range of Light." To meet this demand, we have undertaken this guide series. The purpose of each book in the series is threefold: first, to provide a reliable basis for planning a trip; second, to serve as a field guide while you are on the trail; and third, to stimulate you to further field investigation and background reading. In each guide, there are a minimum of 100 described miles of trails, and the descriptions are supplemented with maps, profiles and other logistical and background information. HIGH SIERRA HIKING GUIDES are based on first-hand observation. There is absolutely no substitute for walking the trails, so we walked all the trails.

In planning this series, we chose the 15-minute quadrangle as the unit because — though every way of dividing the Sierra is arbitrary — the quadrangle map is the chosen aid of almost every wilderness traveler. Inside the back cover of this book is a map of the quadrangle, showing described trails and mileages accurately. With this map, you can always get where you want to go, with a minimum of detours or wasted effort.

Left: Looking south down the Kern River Canyon.

One other thing the wilderness traveler will need: a permit from the Forest Service (for Federally designated wilderness areas) or from the National Park Service (for national-park back country). The two services reciprocally honor each others permits, so if your hike goes from one to the other, get your permit at an office of the agency that administers the area where you will start. For eastside entrance into the *Mt. Whitney* quad, write Mt. Whitney Ranger Station, P.O. Box 8, Lone Pine, CA 93545. (The station is on Highway 395 at the south edge of town.) For westside entrance, write Sequoia-Kings Canyon National Park, Three Rivers, CA 93271. Or you can call (916) 876-5542. There are strict quotas on the Mt. Whitney Trail, which are filled very early.

No guns or dogs are allowed on trails in Sequoia National Park or Kings Canyon National Park. Some areas have restricted entry seasons in order to protect the herds of bighorn sheep there (see the end of the chapter "The Fauna" and the map).

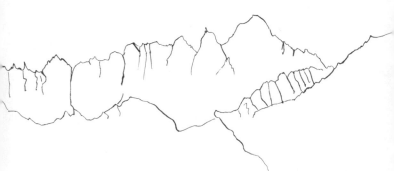

Table of Contents

The Country

MOST PEOPLE WHO come to the *Mt. Whitney* quadrangle do so in order to climb Mt. Whitney. In coming only for this purpose, they miss out on some of the finest mountain experiences to be had anywhere in the world. This quadrangle contains the highest, wildest parts of the entire High Sierra. Only one road is shown anywhere on the map, and it barely pierces the northeast boundary. A gigantic horseshoe of 13,000′ and 14,000′ peaks protects the heart of this quadrangle from the incursions of casual campers and day-walkers.

Inside the horseshoe is the high plateau where the Kern River has its sources. Like an equine foot, this horseshoe is cleft down its center by the great trench of the Kern River, as deep as Yosemite Valley, not much wider, and very much longer. The erosive power of water and ice found a receptive channel here along a great, straight-line earthquake fault in the earth's crust. The Kern River, unlike all other Sierra Nevada rivers, which flow *west* down the slope from the crest, flows south for over 70 miles before finally finding a way over to the San Joaquin Valley, where its waters are diverted into irrigation ditches.

The east side of the horseshoe is the climax of the Sierra crest, with four 14,000′ peaks, from Mt. Tyndall on the north to Mt. Muir on the south. The top of the horseshoe is the Kings-Kern divide, notched by Forester Pass, the last and

Mt. Williamson basin (left) is the least-visited part of this quadrangle. The view from an airplane shows, from left to right in the middle ground, Mt. Williamson, Trojan Peak, Mt. Barnard and Mt. Tyndall. At the very top is the Kern River Canyon.

highest pass along the John Muir Trail for those walking south. The western arm of the horseshoe, culminating in 13,802′ Mt. Kaweah, seals off this Shangri La basin from the lower, gentler western Sierra slopes.

Only five maintained trails give access to this wilderness, and of these only three cross the great horseshoe anywhere around its arc. But the lover of high country does not lobby for more trail-building, and often prefers to enter the upper Kern Basin via some favorite cross-country route hidden among the granite pinnacles and talus slopes. Lovers of high country rate the Mt. Whitney quad "tops," and if we can ignore the claims of that distant state acquired from the Russians, it is indeed the top of the United States.

The History

THE YEAR WAS 1864, THE place was the uncharted Sierra wilderness.

> To the south, more than eight miles away, a wall of peaks stood across the gulf, dividing the Kings, which flowed north at our feet, from the Kern River, that flowed down the trough in the opposite direction.
>
> I did not wonder that Brewer and Hoffman pronounced our undertaking impossible; but when I looked at Cotter there was such complete bravery in his eye that I asked him if he was ready to start. His old answer, "Why not?" left the initiative with me; so I told Professor Brewer that we would bid him good by. Our friends helped us on with our packs in silence, and as we shook hands there was not a dry eye in the party. Before he let go of my hand, Professor Brewer asked me for my plan, and I had to own that I had but one, which was to reach the highest peak in the range.

The writer was Clarence King, the peak was Mt. Whitney, and King did reach the top, but only 9 years later, after he had climbed two peaks each of which he thought to be the highest until after he had climbed it.

Clarence King was a member of the California State Geological Survey, an intrepid mountaineer, and a writer of hair-raising prose. The survey, created by the State Legislature in 1860, was under the direction of Josiah D. Whitney. A field trip to the uncharted southern Sierra in 1864 was under the leadership of William Brewer; Charles Hoffman was the cartographer, King and James Gardiner were assistant geologists, and Dick Cotter was their packer.

King and Cotter entered the *Mt. Whitney* quadrangle on the northwest, at the saddle south of Mt. Brewer, and thus began the first recorded exploration of our quad. They crossed the mighty Kings-Kern Divide, risking their lives in the doing, somewhere in the headwaters of East Creek. No one knows exactly where, but an educated guess is the saddle immediately east of Thunder Mountain.

Once over this divide, they set out for Mt. Tyndall, named by King when he arrived at its summit. But then he saw there were two peaks higher than this one. They were, of course, Mt. Williamson and Mt. Whitney. Of the latter, King said, "That which looked highest of all was a cleanly cut helmet of granite, lying about six miles south. Mount Whitney, as we afterwards called it in honor of our chief, is probably the highest land within the United States. The summit looks glorious, but inaccessible."

Since their provisions and Cotter's shoes were both about gone, they returned to Brewer's camp in the Roaring River watershed. But King was obsessed with climbing Whitney. A few days later, he set off from Visalia and crossed the range to a point south of Whitney and east of the main crest. After several days of exploration in unmapped, unknown, extremely rugged country, King got to within three or four hundred feet of the summit before being defeated. Again he called the summit "inaccessible."

The work of the Survey kept King away from the Whitney area for the next few years, but in June 1871 he was himself in charge of a geological survey. While returning to his party in Wyoming from San Francisco, he detoured south to Lone Pine for another chance at the unclimbed giant. And, via a new route, he gained the summit. At last he had his first ascent, and the accolades it brought him.

But two years later a scientist by the name of W. A. Good-year proved simply and conclusively that King had been, not on Whitney, but on a peak about 6 miles south — now called Mt. Langley. The real Whitney, which King had seen from Tyndall, remained unclimbed. King, getting the news in the East, immediately set out for California. This time he did indeed reach the summit of the real Mt. Whitney. But as he discovered in records he found on top, he was not the first.

A mere 13 days after Goodyear had made his statement, on August 18,1873, three fishermen had climbed Whitney, from their base camp at Soda Springs on the Kern River. Little publicized since, they were John Lucas, Charles Begole and Albert Johnson. Late in August a second party surmounted the highest peak, and in early September a third. King came on September 19.

Just a month later came a man now more familiar than King or any other Sierra explorer: John Muir. As usual, he went alone, finding a route up a couloir on the northeast side.

By 1881, the summit was being used for scientific observations, but staying all night on the summit even in August was too arduous, and the party's leader said a permanent shelter would have to be constructed. A stock trail was needed, too, and this the citizens of Lone Pine completed in 1904. The stone structure that stands on Whitney today was built in 1909, and scientists made expeditions to the summit in 1909, 1910 and 1913. Since then, other high places, such as Pikes Peak, have been made more easily accessible, and scientists on Whitney these days are there for nonprofessional reasons — although they are not above sleeping in the shelter if they choose to spend the night on top.

Of course, Mt. Whitney is no longer the highest in the U. S. — McKinley is. And the often-read statement that it is now second highest is wrong by 14 peaks; there are 15 higher in Alaska.

The west "half" of the zero-dimensional pinpoint that theoretically marks the summit of Mt. Whitney is in Sequoia National Park, and has been since 1926. The park was created in the same year as Yosemite, 1890, but it was much smaller until Congress in 1926 added the part that is in the Kern River watershed.

Exploration of the rest of the *Mt. Whitney* quadrangle languished from the time Brewer's party left until roughly the 1890s, when early Sierra Club people, having worked their way, summer by summer, south from Yosemite reached the Kings-Kern Divide. Bolton Coit Brown, a Professor of Drawing at Stanford, scrambled over the peaks and ridges here, sketching and mapping what he saw. For years, his sketches were the only useful maps of some of the area. With his wife Lucy he went over the pass which bears her name, and she seems to have gone just about everywhere he did. On their third summer-long trip, they brought their 2-year-old daughter on a mule.

In 1908 Joseph N. LeConte and two companions took pack animals from Tuolumne Meadows to the South Fork of the Kings River via a route that the present John Muir Trail more or less follows. This super-trail was completed in 1938 with the building of the Mather Pass segment (off our quad), but by 1932, with the opening of Forester Pass, there was a continuous, maintained route from Yosemite Valley to Mt. Whitney.

The future of this quad is quite conjectural. Most of it is so remote that overuse would seem to be far in the future. But backpacking in the Sierra in recent years has had a compound growth rate of about 18%. At this rate, the amount of use doubles in four years. Some kind of control is being discussed by the national park and national forest authorities. One obvious way to control is to limit access, using required permits as the device. Permits have now become a reality. Another kind of control involves building facilities such as rest rooms and restaurants. For example, Forest Service authorities may seek to remove the Mt. Whitney trail from its present wilderness status, in order to permit some construction.

But there is some question whether it is possible by definition to "manage a wilderness." Better alternatives must exist, and it behooves the dedicated backpacker to think through them, and propose his best ideas to all who will listen.

Mountain chickadee

The Sierra escarpment (Mt. Whitney right of center)

The Geology

WHEN WE APPROACH the *Mt. Whitney* quadrangle via the highway on the east side of the mountains, we are astounded and awestruck by the sheer, towering, grand eastern scarp of the Sierra. How could such a fabulous scarp have been created?

Almost every part of the continental crust has been beneath the sea many times since the oceans were formed. In the Sierra, each time this happened, river-borne sediments and the products of volcanic eruptions piled up on the sinking sea floor to depths of more than 5 miles. Later, the accumulated piles were broken and crumpled, then altered by heat and pressure to hard crystalline rock, and eventually raised above the sea. The new land thus created was eroded by water and wind, and after many eons it finally sank under the sea. These great cyclical earth processes were repeated again and again in the area we call the Sierra.

Then, during several periods of uplift, lasting from about 200 million to 80 million years ago, huge fingers of molten granite invaded the strata from below and solidified deep within the crust to form bodies of granitic rock.

In the last 80 million years erosion has taken away something like 9 vertical miles of rock, thus exposing granite over most of the range. Many people, in fact, think of the Sierra as being all granite — though as we shall see it is not.

Between 10 and 15 million years ago, upthrusting forces began to raise the Sierra to its present height. Initially, the land to the east rose right along with the Sierra, creating a broad arch that extended east many miles beyond the present crest. Later, beginning about 9 million years ago, but mainly

between 7 and 2 million years ago, the land to the east of
the present Sierra dropped thousands of feet while the Sierra
block stayed high — or even continued to rise. At the inter-
face between the two great blocks, huge faults developed. Dis-
location along these faults proceeded at the rate of only a
fraction of an inch per year, but in a few million years this
movement had created a fault scarp 10,000 feet high. The
fault scarp was eroded back as the land to the east dropped
away, to form the rugged east face of the Sierra we now see.

About 3 million years ago, the Sierra experienced the first
of many ice ages. By this time the range was high enough, and
hence cold enough, for ice to exist the year around. However,
glaciers more than a million years old existed in only a few
places in the Sierra, and they contributed little to the present
sculpture of the range. But within the last million years, ice
fields that formed around the summits of the range grew and
merged until they covered an area about 270 miles long and
20-30 miles wide, except for the higher peaks and divides. This
is the area we call the High Sierra.

This glacial ice sculptured the landscape we see today as
we walk the trails of the *Mt. Whitney* quadrangle. The glaciers simply took the rock from one place and put it in
another. The power they had was great enough to make
big canyons out of little ones, to tear down mountain peaks,
and to scoop out lake basins hundreds of feet deep. The steep
peaks and divides that characterize this quadrangle are the
result of glaciers "eating" headward at the upper ends of their
valleys. Above the ice surface, frost-wedging pries chunks of
rock out of the steep mountainside by alternately freezing and
thawing the water that seeps into tiny cracks in the rock. The

pried-out boulders tumble down onto the ice at the upper end of the glacier. Beneath the ice, at the bottom of the large crevass that develops at the head of any glacier, similar freezing and thawing loosens blocks of rock, and then the moving ice pulls them out and carries them away. This process is called *quarrying*.

The amphitheaterlike bowl that a glacier creates in its upper reaches is called a *cirque*. Two cirques being eroded headward toward the divide that separates them eventually create a knifelike ridge called an *arete;* three or more create a spiry peak called a *horn*.

By frost-wedging and quarrying, a glacier acquires a set of cutting and grinding tools — great rocks frozen into its bottom and sides — which it uses to abrade the canyon down which it flows. If the bedrock underneath is extensively *jointed* (laced with cracks), the glacial erosion will create a valley that is U-shaped in cross section, like the Kern River trench. A combination of quarrying and abrasion beneath the ice deepens the canyon and cuts off the spurs of side canyons. If, on the other hand, the rock is what geologists call *massive,* meaning unjointed, it will resist the attacks of the glaciers. It is not susceptible to the ice-cracking, lifting and plucking by which glaciers do their work. The presence of such rock accounts for valleys that remain V-shaped. In such places, glacial erosion was restricted primarily to rasping and polishing because it simply couldn't get a "bite" into the massive, unjointed rock facade presented to the ice.

At the lower end of the glacier, supply and demand are equal: the rate at which flowing ice arrives there just balances the rate of melting, and, as economists would tell us, there is *equilibrium.* When the terminal ice melts, it drops its load of rock, gravel, sand and silt, and they form a terminal moraine. The glacier has already dropped some of its load along its side margins, forming lateral moraines. And when the climate warms and the glacier recedes back into the highlands, it drops the rest of its load right where it melts, forming a ground moraine. Meanwhile, the receding glacier may temporarily stop melting several times; each time another terminal moraine will be laid down. Unlike sedimentary deposits in bodies of water, glacial deposits are not sorted according to particle size and are not laminated into beds.

In the Sierra there were at least four glacial stages, separated by periods during which the climate was warmer than it is today. The last stage reached its peak about 20,000 years ago, and ended only 9500 years ago. By that time, all the glaciers had melted. The ones we see today have been formed in the last 4000 years, due to a recent cooling of the climate. However, the *most* recent trend has been a warming one, so that the glaciers are only about half as big as they were 100 years ago. Given such fast geological action, the guides in this series may need frequent revision!

"Let us, while waiting for new monuments, preserve the old monuments..."   Victor Hugo

The Fauna

EACH GUIDE IN THIS SERIES will acquaint the reader with some of the animals he may meet in the quadrangle, rather than try to give a too-brief overall summary of the fauna.

The remote country of *Mt. Whitney* quad is one of the last places in the world where one may still see a wolverine. It is an endangered species, to say the least, and the reason is simply the spread of man. If species persisted in proportion to their endurance, tenacity and ferocity, wolverines might have inherited the earth. Bears and mountain lions, even when in pairs, have been seen to back away from their meal and yield possession of it to an approaching wolverine.

Yet this animal is no longer than a poodle, and not so tall. A large one weighs but 30 pounds. Zoologists can't explain their power. Some have mentioned thyroid glands or adrenalin secretion, but very tentatively. Perhaps it will remain unexplained, except in the heart of the wolverine.

A member of the weasel family, the wolverine has evolved into a chunky, powerful animal capable of traveling long and far through deep snow. It can live in such a harsh environment that it has almost no competitors, the climate itself being the chief enemy. When the snow lies deep, and the small rodents are hibernating under it, the wolverine must range far and wide to get enough to subsist, and he must eat anything, dead or alive, that he can find. He must also be able to go for long periods without eating, and so has developed such an ability to gorge himself that some people call him the "glutton."

If you should be so lucky as to see a wolverine, you would probably not mistake him for anything else, except possibly a young bear. However, his legs are shorter than a bear's, and the tail is large and bushy. Mostly brownish black, he has two big brownish-gray stripes extending from the shoulders to the base of the tail, and a gray bar across the forehead.

More likely — but not commonly — you might see the wolverine's tracks. They may look like a coyote's or mountain lions' if the fifth toe on the forefoot hasn't made a clear impression.

Wolverine

A mammal you are much more likely to see in this quad is the cony, or as some call him the pika. Having the head of a rat, the body and fur of a rabbit, and no visible tail, the cony presents a curious appearance. We find it at elevations of 8000-12000′, living in colonies. One colony was observed living in a rockslide covering more than an acre of ground, a conglomerated mass many feet deep, with blocks of rock ranging from a few inches to many feet in diameter, thus providing ample shelter with many crevices as runways. Among the cracks of this slide the conies have built their home, and they forage for herbs and grasses growing around the nearby lakes. The lower part of the slide extends well out into the lake, so the animals can obtain drink during the winter without exposing themselves on top of the snow to bad weather or predators.

Conies are of social and affectionate disposition, and notwithstanding their wild, free life on the edge of timberline in the solitudes of the High Sierra, they seem to be holding their own and increasing in number. Their haymaking season is between August 20 and September 15, varying somewhat with altitude and the ripening condition of the grasses. Practically all members of the colony take part in the harvest. The one object is to store sufficient hay to last over the winter. This is no small task, as the winters often last 8 months, and snow is 10-30′ deep over all vegetation. The conies with their strong incisor teeth cut off the grass close to the roots and then place it carefully in small bunches for drying. Then they take the sheaves of hay, throw them over their shoulders, and drag them to the "haybarns" under the rocks. With their snouts and front feet, the little animals force the sheaves of cured grass back into crevices.

"The conies are a little folk, but they build their homes among the rocks." The psalmist

From the appearance of the hayfield after the harvest season, some people believe that the animals shear off more grass than they want, but the remains are usually hay that has been damaged in the curing process by mountain storms.

The cony is very agile, and can run like a rat and jump like a rabbit. In bounding from rock to rock when closely pursued, he can spring several feet, though only 7″ long. Conies hate to get into deep water, but in an emergency they can swim fast for up to 60 feet. They are home-loving, with little migratory impulse other than to search for fresh pasture when unfavorable forage conditions arise or find a new home when forced abroad by congested living conditions. Their worst enemies are the weasel and some hawks.

Once you see these animals you'll have a desire for more acquaintance, for the little cliff-dwellers are curious and interesting from many points of view. Their industry excels that of most animals; they are home-loving, always living in family groups; the sexes are almost alike in size and color; they do not hibernate. Conies appear to be a very ancient mammal that has been able to live in a habitat difficult for other animals to utilize.

The long-tailed weasel in his white winter coat is sometimes called ermine, but "ermine" is also the name of the short-tailed weasel, or least weasel, the smallest carnivore in the Sierra. The ermine is a little animal not much bigger than a big mouse, drab-brown upper body, black-tipped tail, and white underparts and feet. He inhabits the Sierra above 6000′ up to timberline, but he is rarely seen anymore — like so many other mammals. His den is a tiny burrow under a rock or tree root.

It is difficult to imagine the capacity for predation shown

by this small animal; its marked intelligence crowns the diminutive weasel as the king of all rodent-killers in the Sierra. One female with six young was observed for 27 days, during which she killed 78 mice, 27 gophers, 2 moles, 34 chipmunks, 3 wood rats and 4 ground squirrels.

This animal is about 9″ long overall, of which about 2″ is tail. Like the long-tailed weasel, it also turns white in winter.

The bighorn sheep, once widespread in the Sierra, is now found mainly in four rather small areas near the crest in the southern High Sierra. One of these is around Mt. Williamson, in our quad, and the sheep living there are called the Mount Williamson herd.

In 1966 the California bighorn sheep *(Ovis canadensis)* was classified as a rare animal within the continental United States. The classification was based largely on a zoologist's 1948-49 studies of the animals, in which he found about 390 sheep in five herds in the Sierra. In the late 1960's the Forest Service conducted extensive field surveys on the sheep ranges to determine what changes had occurred since the previous studies. It found that the number of bighorn sheep had continued to decline — although the Mt. Williamson herd had remained fairly static. The Forest Service said the decline was *not* due to illegal hunting, accidental death, predation, internal parasites or diseases, nor to forage competition between bighorns and domestic livestock. Rather, the depressants on the size of bighorn herds were forage competition on the winter range with deer and tule elk, and particularly the great increase in human use on the bighorn ranges.

In 1971 the Forest Service created a California bighorn sheep zoological area of two separate pieces: a total of 40,400 acres on the east slopes of Mt. Williamson and of Mt. Baxter (in *Mt. Pinchot* quadrangle and the home of the Mt. Baxter herd). To give top priority to protecting the bighorn sheep, the Forest Service will not construct new trails in the area (see map in inside back pocket) and will maintain existing trails only minimally. In some parts of the area (see map) human travel is restricted and overnight camping is prohibited. The area has been withdrawn from mineral entry, and other regulations have been imposed to help protect these last refuges of these marvelous animals. The backpacker can do his bit for *Ovis canadensis* by observing the regulations.

The Flora

SIMPLY LISTING THE FLOWERS of a given area may be a way of communicating with botanists, but hardly with laymen. These guides, not being compiled for the professional botanist, will contain no such lists. Instead, each one will introduce the casual flower-lover (or liker) to some of the floral delights of the High Sierra. *Mt. Whitney* quadrangle is a good place to see flowers that grow only at high elevations, and this chapter will describe three of them.

Polemonium, or sky pilot *(Polemonium eximium)*. One has to climb very high to find this beautiful plant, for it grows far above timberline, and seldom below 11500′, on the high peaks of the Sierra Nevada crest from Tuolumne County to Tulare and Inyo counties.

Intoxicating perfume permeates the thin air where sky pilot

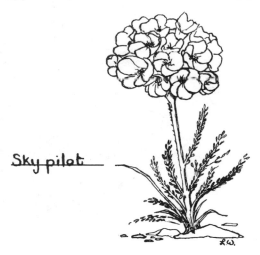

Sky pilot

grows upright and tall despite the extreme physical conditions it must live under. Its loosely clustered multiple flowers, source of the perfume, are a luminous blue. The plant is justly famous among Sierra Club members as a symbol of mountaineering achievement, and tradition once decreed that one very tiny sprig of this lovely plant might be picked and worn in the hatband of the mountaineer who had climbed a peak of 13000′ or higher.

Alpine gold, or alpine sunflower *(Hulsea algida)*. Alpine gold, along with sky pilot, grows tall and straight on the summits of the Sierra's highest peaks, where other plants lie prostrate and clinging to the scant shelter of the exposed rocky substratum. What a pair! Sky pilot and alpine gold! The

alpine gold

gloriously golden color of Hulsea's huge sunflower heads con-
trasts vividly with the intense blue of sky pilot's flowers. Nature, however, has distributed both of these magnificent plants
sparingly. They occur on almost every high peak, yet the
individual plants are scattered and often quite distant from
one another. Hulsea, unlike sky pilot, ranges far beyond the
Sierra into other western alpine areas, but its charm for the
Sierra mountaineer is, nonetheless, second only to sky pilot's.

Alpine phlox *(Phlox caespitosa* subsp. *pulvinata, Phlox co-
villei,* and *Phlox dispersa).* Several very similar kinds of alpine
phlox are found above timberline not only in the Sierra but
throughout the west. These small phloxes form extremely con-
densed and compacted plants, which are good examples of
what German botanists call "polster" (cushion) plants. Quite
unrelated kinds of arctic and alpine plants living under the
severe conditions of high latitude or high altitude frequently
have this same type of growth. The heavy, woody roots of
polster plants, including those of alpine phloxes, may grow
to an amazing length and size, anchoring the plant against the
violent winds, and extending deep and wide to gather the scant
moisture so vital for combatting the desiccating influences of
the dry air and low temperatures. These roots also furnish
storage space for reserve food to tide the plant over the long
winter season of dormancy. Yet all that appears above ground
may be a small, dense mat of leaves and stems pressed together very tightly into a ball or cushion perhaps only one or
two inches high.

No icy gale can tear so much as a leaf from a well-armored
polster plant, nor penetrate that armor and still have any
strength left. In a relenting mood, however, nature frequently

supplies such a sternly frocked plant with a myriad of beautiful blossoms during its brief flowering season. This is what
happens to our alpine phloxes. The plant may be quite liter-
ally covered with small, exquisite, white or pale lavender
flowers, and not a harsh leaf or stem be seen beneath this
delicate and wonderfully fragrant mound.

Alpine phlox

The Climate

TO THE BACKPACKER, weather is as important as cards are to a gambler. And in fact it is something of a gamble whether one's trip will be sunny and clear, or wet and cold. Fortunately, in the *Mt. Whitney* quadrangle, the odds are very much in one's favor.

The Sierra Nevada has indisputably the finest climate of any mountain range in America. Only 3% of the year's precipitation falls during the summer. As for warmth, the average daily maximum at 10000′ in summertime is only about 60°—but no one experiencing the delicious warmth of the direct sunlight in the high country believes that, unless he consults a thermometer. At night in the summer, the temperature usually drops to 40° or less, and freezes are not uncommon, but the dryness of the air (augmented by a good sleeping bag) minimizes the feeling of cold. Many High Sierra veterans, in fact, prefer a little frost to wake up to; lying in the sack watching the bright early sun play on a whitened granite slope or meadow is an ineffable experience.

When a thunderstorm does come to *Mt. Whitney* quad, the lightning which generally precedes and follows the storm is a danger to be reckoned with. The best rule of thumb in such situations is to avoid being conspicuous and avoid being near conspicuous landmarks. A dense grove of uniformly sized trees is a good place. The most dangerous places are on ridges, under lone trees, and on or beside open expanses of water. Climbers working on exposed surfaces should keep a particularly wary eye on the weather, and plan their climbs accordingly.

But to precede the traveler's visit to *Mt. Whitney* with dire warnings and a list of do's and don't's is to destroy that prized and terribly fragile element of the wilderness experience called *discovery*. We go to wilderness to discover what is there to be seen and felt; we abandon our defenses against the machines that we left back in Gross National Productland, and listen to the silence. In a few days, we get an inkling of what things matter.

"Survival is not enough. Seeing the Milky Way, experiencing the fragrance of spring and observing other forms of life continue to play an immense role in the development of humanness."   Rene Dubos

The Trails

THE MOST USED TRAILS IN this quadrangle lead to the top of Mt. Whitney—the John Muir Trail coming from the north, and the Mt. Whitney trail coming from the east. The two are superimposed for their last two miles. Although no figures are available, we estimate that 90% of the walking mileage logged in this quadrangle is logged on these two trails. The High Sierra trail and the East Creek trail probably account for more than half of the remaining 10%.

While one cannot deny the appeal and the excitement of these trails, one may want to seek a quieter, less traveled piece of country. For this, the *Mt. Whitney* quadrangle is extremely well suited. Much of it is easily walked off-trail. Above timberline you can see for miles, so route-picking is especially easy. Furthermore, there are fairly large areas of high plateau, where grades are easy. It is possible to spend a month in the trailless high country, every night at a different campsite if you so choose, with little likelihood of seeing anyone else except perhaps from a distance. The authors once spent a week just a mile across gentle slopes from the Muir Trail and saw no one.

Since much of the fun of going cross country comes from finding your own way, the cross-country routes in the descriptions that follow are pointed out only in very general terms. If you have had sufficient experience, you will, with the aid of a map and some advance planning, get where you want to go. One word of caution is in order here: beginners should err on the conservative side while they get the feel of going cross country and camping off trail, and they certainly should not do it alone. A person may have the right to do with his body as he chooses, but he does not have the right to cause others discomfort and worry because he carelessly got lost or hurt.

The route descriptions that follow often mention "ducks" and "cairns." A duck is one or several small rocks placed upon a larger rock in such a way that the placement is obviously not natural. A cairn is a number of small rocks made into a pile.

THE TRAILHEADS

Symmes Creek Roadend. Go 4½ miles west from Independence on the Onion Valley Road; turn left at Foothill Road, and go 1.3 miles to a fork. Take the right-hand fork and go past an old corral on the left, then immediately cross Symmes Creek. In ½ mile take the right fork, and take the right fork again at the next two forks. Then go ½ mile to the trailhead near Symmes Creek. Some of these forks may have small signs. (Access to Shepherd Pass and Junction Pass.)

Whitney Portal. At the end of a 13-mile paved road west from Lone Pine. (Access to Mt. Whitney and John Muir Trail.)

Cedar Grove. At the end of State 180, 85 miles east of Fresno. (Access to Bubbs Creek Trail and thence to Trail #5.)

Trail Descriptions

TRAIL #1

John Muir Trail (31.8 miles)

This long traverse of the Mt. Whitney quadrangle is the climax of the John Muir Trail, terminating at the highest point in the "lower 48" states. We begin the trail description at Vidette Meadow on Bubbs Creek, just off our quadrangle to the north.

From Vidette Meadow the trail makes an initial steep ascent and then resolves into a steady climb along the east bank of the creek, through a moderate forest cover of lodgepole pine and occasional foxtail pine. Several campsites line Bubbs Creek, and some around 10,000′ offer fine campsite views of University Peak to the east, Center Peak to the southeast, and East Vidette to the west.

From those campsites, the trail continues up the east side of dashing Bubbs Creek, passing more campsites bunched around small side streams and then reaching the Center Basin/Junction Pass Trail. Just beyond, the Center Basin outlet stream is a formidable ford in early season. Our route then ascends somewhat steeply over nearly barren granite west of towering Center Peak. This climb takes the panting hiker above timberline as it winds back and forth over the runoff stream that drains Lake 12248. Over one's shoulder, the peaks of the Sierra crest march away on the northern horizon.

After fording just below Lake 12248, the trail doubles back

north on the barren canyon wall and then turns south and soon switchbacks steeply up to a narrow notch in the Kings-Kern Divide called Forester Pass (13180′), the highest pass on the Muir Trail. Views from this windy notch are extraordinary. The entire Palisade Crest is in view to the northwest. To the north and east are Mt. Pinchot, University Peak, Mt. Bradley and Mt. Keith. In the south (reading clockwise) are Mt. Guyot, Mt. Kaweah and the Kaweah Peaks Ridge, the Red Spur, Kern Point, Black Kaweah and Red Kaweah.

Leaving this windy notch behind, the trail descends steeply by numerous switchbacks, some of which are mere shelves carved into the steep face of Junction Peak's west shoulder. A few hardy flowers called polemonium and alpine gold (see the chapter "Flora") share the high slope with scurrying conies (see the chapter "Fauna"), and the traveler who lifts his eyes is sometimes treated to the sight of a golden eagle soaring high above the granite peaks. After the trail becomes less steep, our rocky route winds among a number of unnamed, rockbound lakes at the headwaters Tyndall Creek. Some of these lakes may still be frozen in August. To the east the unusual formation called Diamond Mesa appears as a sheer-walled, flat-topped ridge protruding from the jumbled heights of Junction Peak. Even here, the barren rock is relieved by occasional flowers of yellow ivesia, red mountain heather and lavender pussypaws, and marmots hop to their dens as we approach.

Near timberline, our route passes a trail that soon splits, the branches leading to Lake South America and to Milestone Creek. A short descent brings us to a junction with the Shepherd Pass Trail, near which a long series of heavily used campsites is strung out along Tyndall Creek.

Then we ford the creek (difficult in early season) and soon pass an unsigned junction with a trail leading down the valley of Tyndall Creek to the Kern River. Beyond this second junction, our route ascends moderately on a rocky slope under a broken forest cover of lodgepole pines. At the unnamed lake northeast of Tawny Point, there are good campsites and great views, and unfreezing swimming.

As we pass through the immense talus slope of Tawny Point, the tree cover changes to foxtail pine, a fascinating species found mainly in the high southern Sierra near timberline. From here, a gentle, sandy ascent leads to a barely perceptible summit on Bighorn Plateau. About ½ mile before the summit, we can look south along the crest of the Tyndall Creek glacier's lateral moraine. (The moraine even shows up on the topo map, as a compressed Z curve on the 11200' contour line.) The view from the trail approaching Bighorn Plateau is one of the finest along the entire Muir Trail, and the lensman may wish to snap a series of frames that scan the horizon from Mt. Kaweah to Junction Peak, later to assemble them into a 180° panorama. The unnamed lake on the summit of the plateau, lying west of the trail across a grassy field, is itself quite photogenic in the morning hours. From the summit the hiker southbound on the Muir Trail has his first view of the terminus of this famous trail — Mt. Whitney.

From this plateau the sandy trail descends via several steps to the glacial moraine that covers the valley of Wright Creek. In the meadow we overlook, a trail of use can be found which goes up the watershed to a dozen high, wild lakes. The highest lake is especially recommended for both fishing and beauty. It is a classic cirque lake, close under 14000' Mt. Tyndall. However, there is no wood. Fair campsites may be found about $1\frac{1}{2}$ miles downstream in the grove of foxtail pines between the words "Wright" and "Lakes" on the topo map. When we walk back down this valley, we are tracing the route Clarence King took on his descent from Mt. Tyndall (see "History").

Another cross-country route also starts here — the shortcut to the Wallace Creek trail. The route turns east from the Muir Trail at the west moraine in Wright Creek valley, crosses a little meadow, goes through a saddle in a moraine on the east side of the valley, and then heads toward the cascades of Wallace Creek, visible in the east. There it joins Trail #10.

Continuing south on the Muir Trail, we pass a good campsite at the ford of Wright Creek (difficult in early season). Then our sandy trail descends to a forested flat about $\frac{1}{2}$ mile long, with a rather dense growth of lodgepole and foxtail pine. At the end of this flat is a photographer's overlook, where excellent pictures may be taken of the Great Western Divide. Then the trail descends steadily to Wallace Creek and a junction with the High Sierra Trail arriving from Giant Forest.

There are fair campsites near the ford (highly difficult in early season). Then the trail switchbacks steeply $\frac{1}{2}$ mile up the south wall of Wallace Creek canyon over rocky going, lightly forested by lodgepole, whitebark and foxtail pine. The ascent becomes less steep where we ford an unnamed tributary and climb for another $\frac{1}{3}$ mile. Then our route rounds the ridge up which we have been climbing, and passes above a pretty little lake in a meadow. Continuing our gentle climb on mostly sandy trail, we ford another runoff stream and enter a foxtail forest on a rocky hillside. From here, views to the north are good of Mt. Ericsson, Tawny Point, Junction Peak, Mt. Tyndall, Mt. Versteeg, Mt. Williamson and Mt. Barnard.

Leveling off, the sandy trail winds below the huge boulders of a glacial moraine on the northwest slope of Mt. Young. From here we make a gentle traverse up to a saddle where the topo map says "BM 10964," and there is a bench mark at that elevation. From the saddle, a simple descent brings us through a sloping meadow, then a foxtail-pine forest, and then the gravelly slope called "Sandy Meadow" on the topo map. Where we cross little runoff streams, we may pause, dazzled by the intense yellow fields of groundsel and monkey flowers. From the second major ford beyond the saddle, we ascend for several hundred feet to an almost level trail section on a boulder-strewn slope dotted with foxtail pines. Because of their leaning tips and narrow profiles, these pines could almost pass for mountain hemlocks. On an overcast day, this foxtail forest, with its dead snags, fallen trees and lack of ground cover, has an eerie, gloomy, otherworldly quality.

On this level portion, we meet a junction from which the Pacific Crest Trail continues south to Crabtree Meadows, and we turn left (east). In a moment the broad back of Mt. Whitney comes into view, and we switchback down to a sandy flat where there is another often-gloomy foxtail forest. As we approach Whitney Creek, lodgepole pines replace foxtails and we come to a junction with another trail to Crabtree Meadows. Across the creek, near the ranger station (emergency services available) are some good campsites in a meadow. During the busy season in late July and August, one may find more secluded camping at Upper Crabtree Meadow (½ mile south of the ranger station) or Lower Crabtree Meadow (1 mile south).

After passing the ranger station and a number of signs indicating what is and is not permitted in the area, we ascend the narrowing canyon of Whitney Creek under a sparse forest cover of lodgepole and foxtail pine. In a meadow where two streams flow together, about ½ mile from the ranger station, are the last campsites below timberline. Ahead, Timberline Lake, though somewhat wooded, is closed to camping. It is, however, a fine spot for a rest stop, and the bulk of Mt. Whitney mirrored in the lake is quite photogenic.

From Timberline Lake we climb rather stiffly, veering away from Whitney Creek and leaving timber behind. Topping a gentle ridge, we descend to ford the inlet of Guitar Lake, where some hikers bound for Mt. Whitney choose to sleep after cooking dinner lower down. Now we veer southward, close under the mighty backside of Mt. Whitney, with excellent views of the avalanche-scarred north face of Mt. Hitchcock. The avalanche chutes end partway down the face; their lower portions were smoothed off by the passage of the most recent glacier, and have not had time to redevelop since then.

Near a meadowy lakelet the climb steepens; then it levels off momentarily, and we can more or less catch our breath for the final assault on the 1500 vertical feet of switchbacks. On this climb, large yellow flowers called hulsea, or alpine gold, have anchored themselves in the most unlikely-looking places. The population pressure on this trail is evidenced by the frequent bedsites constructed in the granite wall, especially near switchbacks.

At 13500′ we meet the Mt. Whitney trail, coming up from Whitney Portal on the east side. Here our route, the John Muir Trail, turns left and begins the last two slogging miles to the summit of Mt. Whitney. As we wind among the large blocks of talus, we often have views, through notch-windows, of Owens Valley, 10000′ below us in the east. Closer below are the heads of barren glacial cirques, most of them containing brilliant turquoise lakes.

Finally, we see ahead on an almost level plateau a small cabin near the summit, and with a well-earned feeling of accomplishment we take the last few steps to the highest point in the "lower 48" states. The view from here is not indescribable — it has been described many times — but the authors prefer to let you see it with fresh eyes, unbiased by what they might say about it.

TRAIL #2

Shepherd Pass Trail (17 miles)

This long, steep trail is only for those in top condition. Their reward is a fast entrance into unpopulated high country. (Beginning in 1971, a policy of minimum trail maintenance was instituted. Downed trees may be removed and rock slides worked over a bit, but that's all.)

The trail begins at the mouth of Symmes Creek canyon and ascends on the south side of the creek through pinyon pine, sagebrush and, at streamside, alders, willows and cottonwoods. The trail fords the creek four times (fill your container at the fourth), passing clumps of early and mid-season columbines. Beyond the fourth crossing the trail begins a long, gruelling series of rocky switchbacks that climb over 2000 feet to a saddle between Shepherd and Symmes creeks. Around 8000 feet red fir and then silver pine form a moderate forest cover, and the entire hot slope is dotted with sagebrush, mountain mahogany and cream bush.

From the saddle at the head of this slope, the great peak we see to the south is Mt. Williamson, second highest in California — though, surprisingly, it is not on the Sierra crest. The steep, deep gash that contains Shepherd Creek falls away at our feet, and it is an impressive introduction to the immense canyons of the eastern escarpment. From this viewpoint the sandy trail descends moderately over two small ridges high above Shepherd Creek before dropping 500 feet down to a dry creek bed. From here the sunny trail climbs through a burned forest of pinyon pine to arrive at the only year-round water between Symmes Creek and Anvil Camp. Beyond this very welcome water the trail climbs to Mahogany Flat, where there is a poor campsite. At the upper end of this "flat" the trail begins a set of long, brushy switchbacks to gain the elevation of the creek's cascade visible to the southwest.

As the route crosses a large talus slope, the environment changes dramatically within a few hundred feet. The trail thus far has been largely on decomposed granite, and the vegetation generally sparse and desertlike. But as the trail reaches Anvil Camp (10,000') the experienced Sierra traveler suddenly realizes that he is in the *High* Sierra: there is duff, a burbling stream, a campsite, willows, grass, and young lodgepole pines. Only hikers in the best of shape will choose to go over the pass the first day, and not camp here.

From Anvil Camp the trail ascends moderately up rocky slopes on the south side of Shepherd Creek. After a mile the unmaintained trail to Junction Pass turns off to the right. Our route crosses the area labeled "The Pothole" on the topo map, and ascends through large boulders to the giant declivity, below the pass, for which that label should have been reserved:

a gargantuan jumble of great jagged rocks weathered out of the headwall of the cirque. The last 500' ascent to Shepherd Pass (12050') is via switchbacks up a steep scree slope, which often has patches of snow into August.

(A cross-country route to Mt. Williamson basin begins at the pass. This basin, between Mt. Tyndall and Mt. Williamson, is indeed a place to get away from it all. The route strikes out southeast to a saddle northeast of Tyndall and drops down to a lake at 12200', above timberline. The lake to the east of this one has good fishing for rainbow, and some beautiful falls below its outlet, but the route to this lake is quite circuitous, around to the cliffs east of it and then carefully down the steep talus.)

At the summit our route enters Sequoia National Park and begins a descent down a broad, boulder-strewn field to alpine meadows and scattered stands of foxtail pine. Immediately to the south is the northern flank of Mt. Tyndall, northernmost of the "Whitney group" of 14000' peaks. The sky along this crest is a marvelous blue on clear days, and it is fitting that John Tyndall, the English scientist for whom Mt. Tyndall was named, is the man who discovered why the sky is blue! He discovered the scattering of light by particles in the air, noting that the light waves of shortest wave length — the blue end of the spectrum — are scattered the most.

(A good cross-country route to the Wright Lakes leaves our trail at the 11600' level. This route traverses southwest to the saddle between Peak 13540' and Peak 12345', and then goes down the east wall of the cirque that lies south of the saddle. The lake basin is described in Trail #1.)

Our route continues down beside Tyndall Creek, through a vast, boulder-strewn, sloping meadow, the 13000' peaks of the Great Western Divide filling the western horizon. There are trails on both sides of the creek, but the one on the north side is more apparent.

After joining the Muir Trail, we ford Tyndall Creek and stroll south for a few hundred yards, past many heavily used campsites. Then we veer right onto the Tyndall Creek trail and enter a mile-long meadow of uneven width. Soon we pass the patrol cabin shown on the topo map (sometimes manned) and ford the creek. It is wet going around here except in late season, but the wildflowers don't complain—they thrive: aster, buttercup, shooting star, little elephant's head, western wallflower, and much lupine. Fair-to-good campsites may be found on both sides of the ford.

At the end of the meadow we pass a sheepherder's sod-roofed cabin that could provide shelter, and enter moderate-to-dense lodgepole forest cover. The underfooting varies from rock to duff as our route veers right and tops a gentle rise, arriving at the brink of the steep-walled Kern River canyon. Views across the canyon to the Great Western Divide are excellent. From this viewpoint the trail descends steeply via a long series of switchbacks that lead 1200 vertical feet down to the aspen-clad banks of the young Kern River, where we meet Trail #3.

---

1. Some people know the silver pine as the *western white pine*.

TRAIL #3

Kern River-Harrison Pass Trail (22.0 miles)

This long northbound trail leads from the southern border of the quadrangle almost to the northern, ending with a difficult off-trail crossing of the Kings-Kern Divide.

From map's edge the trail ascends gently, sometimes a bit stiffly, beside the Kern River, heading almost due north. The U-shaped trough of the Kern River, called the Kern Trench, is remarkably straight for about 25 miles as it traces the Kern Canyon fault. The fault, a zone of structural weakness in the Sierra batholith, is more susceptible to erosion than the surrounding rock, and this deep canyon has been carved by both glacial and stream action. Three times the glacier advanced down the canyon, shearing off spurs created by stream erosion and leaving some tributary valleys hanging above the main valley. The glacier also scooped and plucked at the bedrock, creating basins in the granite which became lakes when the glacier melted and retreated.

The walls of this deep canyon, from 2000 to 5000 feet high, are quite spectacular, and a number of streams cascade and fall down these walls. (The fords of the stream draining Guyot Flat, Whitney Creek and Wallace Creek can be difficult in early season.) The river is the home of hybrid trout whose origins have been variously interpreted, but whatever their origins, they taste fine, and they are not too hard to catch.

"The only trouble with our time is that the future is not what it used to be."   Paul Valery

Six miles up the trail we come to a Junction Meadow. (Trail #5 starts at another Junction Meadow.) Here a parklike grove of stalwart Jeffrey pines provides a noble setting for a number of good campsites. Beyond this meadow the trail ascends more steeply, up a hillside where the forest cover is mainly aspen with some pines — not dense enough to cut off the excellent view down the canyon. After 1 mile and 800 vertical feet, the sweating hiker appreciates it when the trail begins to level off, roughly at the junction where the High Sierra Trail to Mt. Whitney turns east.

Beginning one mile up the canyon from here, there are several good campsites along the river, where firewood is ample and fishing is good for rainbow.

Once past the campsites, the trail ascends less steeply, and soon it reaches the ford of Tyndall Creek (difficult in early season). Beyond the ford, the trail becomes sandier and drier, and the red fir and aspen gradually disappear, leaving a forest cover of lodgepole and some foxtail that is sparse on the hillsides and moderate on the river terraces. There are numerous campsites along this stretch of trail, including a packer campsite ½ mile beyond the Tyndall Creek trail.

After passing the hard-to-spot Tyndall Creek trail, our route becomes more exposed, with considerable sagebrush. The trail fords the outlet stream of Lake 11440 and soon comes to a dell thick with lodgepole trunks. The wildflower display in this large dell is dominated by yellow groundsel, but includes also orange tiger lilies, purple swamp onion and red columbine. Above the dell, the trail ascends through a bank of shield fern, Queen Anne's lace and bush chinquapin. Then, through a sparse lodgepole cover, our rocky trail ascends 600' up granite slabs to the upper Kern Plateau. The trail levels off and soon passes the unsigned junction with the Milestone Basin trail.

Two hundred yards farther on we come to an unnamed lake at 10700', where a trail to Shepherd Pass branches right. Fishing and camping are good at this crossroads lake, but for solitude and sweeping beauty, the intrepid hiker will continue on to higher lakes.

A short half mile up the river, our route, now near timberline, passes another lake and veers eastward, climbing moderately under a sparse forest cover of lodgepole and whitebark pines. (At the 11000' contour the adventurous backpacker may turn north and curve west around the medium-large lake with three bays on its north side, bound for the high lakes between Table Mountain and Mt. Jordan. It would be hard to find a more remote part of the United States or a finer alpine setting for fishing and for absorbing the unsurpassed views in this upper Kern basin. Little pockets of timber along the creek offer some firewood and some storm protection.)

We continue upward on the indistinct, ducked "trail" in the lake-dotted super-cirque under the Kings-Kern Divide, welcoming the need to pause for breath, as it allows us to look back at the superlative view to the south. Beyond 3 medium-sized lakes, the trail veers eastward and climbs somewhat steeply to a trail junction beside a little lake perched on a hilltop. It is easy to get carried away about this upper Kern country, but this little lake has to be called a jewel, with its preternaturally blue water rimmed along one side by snow the whole summer long, and its bordering clumps of fragile, fragrant, blue polemonium, the favorite flower of many mountaineers.

At the junction we take the signed trail to Lake South America, and very soon arrive at the shallow outlet. Our route, no longer a trail but marked only by ducks, continues north up a gentle slope above timberline. One may lose the ducks from time to time, but more appear as one simply heads for the low point on the divide ahead. All routes in this broad valley are good routes. Near the divide, a trail of use becomes evident again as it climbs eastward to reach the crest east of the lowest point on the saddle. A cairn here marks the proper crossing of Harrison Pass. Views from the pass to the north are interrupted by the bulk of Deerhorn Mountain rising athwart our line of sight, but to the left of it in the distance we can see Mt. Goddard, and to the right, Middle Palisade. In the south, landmarks include Mt. Kaweah, Kaweah Peaks Ridge, Milestone Mountain and Mt. Guyot.

The descent down the north side of the pass is difficult, and should be attempted only by experienced mountaineers, as it may require rope. In some years the snow lies deep on this steep slope all summer long. It is hard to believe that Robert Pike took horses and donkeys northward over the pass (then called Madary's Pass) on July 4, 1901, or that Force Parker took horses southward over the pass two years later. Pike wrote afterward, "On looking down it, we were strongly impressed with the fact that places called 'passes' differ widely in character." As for Parker, his party reached the top at 4 a.m. In any event, the route is Class II, if a rather high II. Keeping to the east side of the bowl, we carefully pick our way downward, toward the first lake visible on the cirque floor. We cross its outlet and veer west to ford the stream connecting the second and third lakes in the cirque. From here

Left: Looking north from Harrison Pass.

the ducked route ascends a few hundred feet and then drops to the outlet of the third lake, passing close under the buff-and-tan granite cliffs of soaring Ericsson Crags. In the canyon below the third lake we encounter timber, and also achieve our first view of Mt. Brewer, due west across the canyon of East Creek. The route then levels off briefly in a meadow and fords the crystal stream to the north side. The white color of the trumpet-shaped flowers of alpine gentian in this meadow tells us we are still quite high; blue gentians lie below. After passing several lovely tarns not shown on the topo map, the ducked and sometimes blazed trail easily crosses a little divide on a southbound course and traverses down to Golden Lake (not named on the map), where there is one excellent campsite and wood is plentiful. From the lake we have a direct view of Lucys Foot Pass, on the Kings-Kern Divide. This pass is Class III in places and it is not advised for ordinary backpacking or for inexperienced mountaineers. Due to all the loose "garbage" on the north side, the best passage is south-to-north.

From Golden Lake the route has a short level segment and then it descends steeply on a rocky-dusty, ill-maintained trail down poorly built switchbacks to the East Creek trail, meeting it at an unsigned junction a few yards north of a talus rockslide.

"The richest values of wilderness lie not in the days of Daniel Boone, nor even in the present, but rather in the future."
                                                          Aldo Leopold

TRAIL #4

Junction Pass Trail to Center Basin (7.5 miles)

This unmaintained trail, once part of the Muir Trail, provides access from the southeast to Center Basin, a beautiful, high basin off the beaten track and little visited. The trail is here described south-to-north, as the shortest access route to Center Basin, but the going is better north-to-south. Access from the north is via Kearsarge Pass.

The Junction Pass trail leaves the Shepherd Pass trail about 1 mile uphill from Anvil Camp, near the confluence of 2 tributaries of Shepherd Creek. The trail is no longer maintained, and is in places hard to follow. Before Forester Pass was completed in 1932, the southbound John Muir Trail ascended Center Basin, crossed Junction Pass, dropped down to the Shepherd Pass trail, and followed it over the Sierra crest to the confluence of the main forks of Tyndall Creek. Following this route, it did not cross but bypassed the Kings Kern Divide.

Leaving the Shepherd Pass trail, we soon pass a lovely subalpine meadow, and then turn westward up a steep slope near timberline. We find the trail at about 11600′, well above timberline, about 300 yards east of the big bend in the unnamed tributary on the topo map. From here we proceed west near the stream for more than a mile along the north slope of the tributary valley. Then, at about 12500′ elevation, our route veers northward and climbs very steeply up a talus slope to the flat saddle northeast of pyramidal Junction Peak.

(If you miss this northward turn, your climb up the talus will be very difficult, and at the head of the canyon it will be impossible.) Views north from the pass (13200') are awe-inspiring, and the sheer east face of Mt. Tyndall in the southeast is a lesson in the process of cirque-formation.

From the pass our route swings west to a ridge that affords a northward way down along a rocky traverse to upper Center Basin. Here, a scant airline mile from the Muir Trail, solitary splendid grandeur rewards the dedicated hiker, and it is only with some regret that he heads on down the basin toward "civilization." He may tarry to climb Center Peak via the east slope or camp on Lake 11776, where campsites are good but wood is unavailable. Approaching the map-indicated Center Basin, the trail levels off and threads a series of alpine, flower-clouded meadows. Golden Bear Lake, in the heart of the basin close under Center Peak, offers some fair campsites on its timbered northern shore. From the lake our trail loops north around several wide places in the creek, and then makes a steepening descent into increasingly dense timber cover. After fording an unnamed tributary amid lush flower gardens, we switchback down to join the Muir Trail at 10500' beside Bubbs Creek.

"If a person lost would conclude that after all he is not lost, he is not beside himself, but standing in his own old shoes on the very spot where he is, and that for the time being he will live there; but the places that have known him, they are lost . . . how much anxiety and danger would vanish."   Henry David Thoreau

TRAIL #5

Junction Meadow on Bubbs Creek to Lake Reflection
(5.0 miles)

This spur trail leads away from the heavily traveled Rae Lakes Loop to a famous lake under the Kings-Kern Divide, a base-camp area for many cross-country adventures.

Our trail starts just off the quad at a Junction Meadow. (Trail #3 passes through another Junction Meadow.) The trail turns south from the Bubbs Creek trail and crosses the creek on a log bridge. Immediately, it begins a switchbacking ascent up a fairly steep slope, sometimes in the forest shade and sometimes in open, sunny enclaves. The trail leaves streamside under red firs but these gradually disappear as we ascend the dry slope, and lodgepole and silver pine become more common.

As the trail ascends through broken granite, brush and grass, one should pause to look back at the deeply fluted south face of Mt. Bago across Bubbs Creek canyon. The grade eases somewhat before we cross East Creek via a log-and-plank bridge. The trail here, a new section built in 1979, stays close to the east bank of tumultuous East Creek. The grade increases before the trail enters a foxtail-pine forest and switchbacks up the east canyon wall. The trail then fords the fern-lined outlet from Lake 11322, where the hiker can pleasure his throat with snowy, clear water and pleasure his eyes with the sight of yellow mimulus and purple monkshood. Beyond this ford the trail tops a slight rise, and we can see East Lake through the trees ahead.

East Lake is a beautiful sight, and good campsites line the north and south shores. This lake is the traditional base for climbing Mt. Brewer, via the east ridge. From the lake's inlet our trail climbs steadily up willowed meadows, their grassy slopes decorated with flowers of pennyroyal, groundsel, sneeze-weed, monkey flower, swamp whiteheads, Indian paintbrush and yarrow milfoil.

About 1 mile from East Lake we pass the unsigned junction with the trail to Harrison Pass (Trail #3). This junction is just before a 50-yard-wide talus rockslide, which we must boulder-hop more or less following a line of ducks. After the rockslide, we pass a number of good campsites beside fish-filled East Creek. The last ½ mile of ascent to Lake Reflection is on a gentle grade through turfy meadow and willow thicket.

There is a large, good campsite beside the lakelet below Reflection, but the best campsites are on the west side of the northernmost bay of the lake. The mirroring reflections from which the lake presumably takes its name are best seen from the granite "beach" here. Firewood is scarce.

However, the lake is the scene of another kind of reflection, which might possibly have led to the naming. When a stormy late-afternoon wind is blowing through the gap west of the lake, one may climb the northwestern shore and witness a re-markable interplay of air, water and light. A gust of wind (heard before it is seen) creates ripples that move across the lake. The same gust is reflected off the steep wall on the other side of the lake, and it then creates other ripples moving in a different direction. The low sun illuminates the differ-ent groups of advancing ripples at different angles, producing a delightful variety of blues, greens and silvery whites. In addi-

tion, the different ripples interfere with each other, producing interference patterns just like the ones studied in optics and hydrodynamics, and these patterns in turn are subjects for magnificent light reflections. Very few lakes have the proper size and setting for these phenomena. Lake Reflection does.

This lake is a traditional base camp for climbing the nearby peaks of the Kings-Kern and the Great Western divides. A trail that ascends southward from the outlet turns into a ducked route over Millys Foot Pass (Class III) and an old trail over Longley Pass can be fairly well followed if one looks for blazes and ducks, beginning on the slopes west of the inlet.

TRAIL #6

From the Muir Trail to the Kern River Trail (3.5 miles)

This trail connects the Muir Trail with the Kern River trail, providing a link in the access to Milestone Basin and other remote country west of the river. It begins ¾ mile north of the Tyndall Creek ford on the Muir Trail.

Following the trail signed *Milestone Creek* and *Lake South America,* this route heads west on nearly level footing across flower-dotted alpine fell fields. After ½ mile, we take the left fork at a Y, leaving the Lake South America trail. Views in this upper Kern Basin are at all times panoramic, and the traveler will mentally record pictures of the skyline that will not soon fade. At the outlet of Lake 11440 the angler can jog northward a short way to sample the good fishing for golden trout. Equally, the knapsacker who likes to camp alone may follow the outlet down for .3 mile to a good campsite beside a grove of foxtail pines near the stream.

From the easy ford of this outlet stream, our trail skirts the north side of a small lake, and makes a short rocky climb to a ridge where the descent to the Kern River begins. From the ridge the traveler has closer views of Mt. Jordan, Thunder Mountain, Milestone Mountain, Midway Mountain, Kern Ridge and Red Spur. The trail descends moderately through rocky and meadowy sections with a moderate cover of high-altitude pines, and arrives at a picturebook lake (you probably have the books) that is fast turning to meadow, geologically speaking. One might regret that all these high lakes are doomed, but one may enjoy the blend of meadows and lakes existing in the time to which he was born.

After climbing slightly from this lake, our route makes a last, steep, dusty descent to the Kern River, where it emerges at an unnamed lake at 10700′ elevation (good fishing for golden and rainbow-golden hybrids to 10″; good camping).

TRAIL #7

From Trail #6 to Trail #3 (2.0 miles)

This trail segment connects Trail #6 with Lake South America, where it meets Trail #3. It provides a shorter way to Harrison Pass from Whitney Portal or Symmes Creek Road-end.

From the Milestone Creek/Lake South America trail junction we ascend gently northward up the east side of a long, boulderstrewn meadow. Two shallow, unnamed lakes in the middle of this meadow have variable borders: in early and mid season, only a detour will prevent wet feet. The silent hiker may be able to approach very close to some of the marmots and conies which claim this rocky upland as their home. Views of the high peaks around Mt. Whitney improve gradually, and then more rapidly as the trail makes a fairly steep 500′ ascent to a saddle which leads to the large cirque basin at the head of the Kern River. About ⅓ mile beyond the saddle, beside one of the prettiest tarns in the entire quadrangle, this route meets Trail #3.

TRAIL #8

Milestone Basin Trail (3.0 miles)

This spur trail leads from the Kern River trail (Trail #3) into the high, beautiful, remote recesses of Milestone Basin.

The unsigned junction where the Milestone trail begins is located about 200 yards down the Kern River trail from the unnamed lake at 10700′ elevation. After fording the river (difficult in early season), the trail contours around to meet Milestone Creek. A campsite here is very unpleasant during the height of the mosquito season. Our route then veers west up a rocky slope away from the creek. After another ½ mile it rejoins the creek at a bench where, besides a waterfall, there is a good campsite. Wood is ample, and fishing in Milestone Creek is good. Views are excellent across the plateau to Mt. Whitney, as they are from so many points in this magnificent high country.

Those who wish to camp as high as possible in the Milestone Basin may climb to the high lake (11900') that lies just to the right of *Midway Mountain* on the topo map. The trail shown on the topo map beside Milestone Creek above the confluence of the north fork does not exist. One should follow the ducked route that turns right up the north fork, passes west through a defile, skirts a small, barren lake and traverses up to the high lake, where fishing is good for golden trout. There are fair campsites with scarce wood below this lake, on the outlet stream.

TRAIL #9

Junction Meadow to Colby Pass (8.5 miles)

This trail leads upward from the Kern River to Colby Pass, a primitive route over the Great Western Divide, on the way to Horse Corral Meadow or Cedar Grove.

This route is unmaintained and impassable to stock, but a knapsacker with any experience will have no trouble staying on the route. Soon after the ford of the Kern River (very difficult in early season) the trail begins the steep ascent up the Kern canyon wall to the hanging valley above. Veering away from the Kern-Kaweah River, it ascends to the north side of a granite knob, or spine, and passes through what has been called "Kern-Kaweah Pass." This difficult climb is repaid by the delightful valley above it, one of the finest in the Sierra. From the "pass" the trail descends very steeply to Rockslide Lake, with its crystal-clear, emerald-green water. (A difficult but thrilling cross-country route to the Chagoopa Plateau goes up the west side of Picket Creek from Rockslide Lake, crossing over to the next creek to the south—unnamed—after climbing out of Kern-Kaweah Canyon. It crosses the divide just east of Mt. Kaweah.)

Just beyond Rockslide Lake the canyon widens into a kind of granite amphitheater, from which we make a steady ascent through a sparse-to-moderate lodgepole cover as the trail threads the deep canyon lying between Kern Point and Picket Guard Peak. One more steep ascent is required to reach the bowl that contains Gallats Lake, really a large meander in a large, wet meadow. Fair campsites are here, but the traveler will prefer those about one mile ahead, where the trail turns away from the stream toward Colby Pass.

Leaving the Kern-Kaweah behind, the trail ascends steeply, and quickly transcends the sparse cover of lodgepole pine. This steep climb offers magnificent views back into the headwaters of the Kern-Kaweah watershed and the background-ing Kaweah Peaks Ridge. Just north of these distinctive summits rise the pyramidal heights of Triple Divide Peak, which trifurcates the drainages of the Kern, Kings and Kaweah rivers. The steepness of the ascent is relieved briefly as we cross the tributaries draining Milestone Bowl. Then, by a faint and unreliably ducked trail, the route resumes its steep climb to Colby Pass (12000'). Here one has grand views down Cloud Canyon and of Glacier Ridge and the cockscomblike sentinels atop Whaleback Ridge. (For the continuation of this trail, see the High Sierra Hiking Guide to *Triple Divide Peak.*)

TRAIL #10

Kern River to Wallace Lake (9.0 miles)

This trail first connects the Kern River trail with the John Muir Trail, and then penetrates the Sierra Crest to a high lake famous for its fishing. It is no longer being maintained.

From a trail junction about 1 mile north of Junction Meadow, our route makes a long, hot, moderately steep traverse toward Wallace Creek canyon. The sparse forest cover of Jeffrey pine and mountain juniper leaves the afternoon hiker mostly exposed, and he should carry water. From this trail, views are excellent down the great Kern River Trench, and lensmen will often stop to select exposures. The granite slopes are well-covered by a number of flowering bushes, including manzanita, creambush, hollyleaf redberry, mountain mahogany and Sierra chinquapin. Shortly after the trail circles left around a ridge, we come upon a single foxtail pine, which will be a first sighting to those who have entered this quadrangle from Giant Forest. Where the trail nears Wallace Creek in its steep-sided canyon, the forest turns to mixed lodgepole and foxtail, moderately spaced. A fair campsite may be found below the trail, near where a bench mark at 9700′ is cemented into a rock on the south side of the trail.

From this plaque, the route makes a moderate ascent through sparse lodgepole to a ford of Wright Creek, then a gentler ascent through denser forest. Fair-to-good campsites are on both sides of the trail here, and the forest scene is considerably brightened by the many hues of fireweed, paintbrush, arnica, sulfur flower, wild buckwheat, pennyroyal, mountain pride and creambush. One more short ascent, on an exposed rocky slope, brings us to a sandy, almost level trail section, and this easy footing lasts for a few hundred yards, to a junction with the John Muir Trail. There are fair campsites, with scarce wood, south of Wallace Creek near the junction.

Continuing up the north side of the creek, our trail (no longer maintained) ascends gently under a cover of sparse-to-moderate lodgepole pine. The shaded forest floor is sprinkled with western wallflower, penstemon, groundsel, yarrow milfoil and Labrador tea. Contrary to the topo-map trail, at the meadow where the outlet of Wales Lake joins Wallace Creek the trail fords Wallace Creek and then fords the tributary, staying on the south side of Wallace Creek. Here the ascent becomes moderate for a short distance, then reverts to a gentler grade. This route up Wallace Creek canyon is sometimes indistinct and sometimes confused by multiple trail sections and inadequate ducking. Careful negotiation of the indistinct sections will bring one to the fair campsites at timberline (11400'), about ½ mile below Wallace Lake, where wood is scarce. Those who prefer to camp at the lake will find sufficient shelter but no wood. Wallace Lake lies in a giant bowl at the foot of the arete that connects Mt. Barnard with Tunnebora Peak, and is a base for the Class I climb of Mt. Barnard. Fishing in Wallace Lake is good for golden, to lunker size, and the same is true of Wales Lake (though the fish are smaller), reached by cross country southwest from the inlet of Wallace Lake.

TRAIL #11

Whitney Portal to the Muir Trail (8.5 miles)

This highly popular, crowded trail provides the one short way from a road to the highest summit in the "lower 48" states. If one is able to postpone one's trip until after Labor Day, it will not be crowded.

From just east of a small store (8361') the route follows the old stock trail from the defunct pack station as it steadily climbs through a moderate forest cover of Jeffrey pine and red fir. After ½ mile the trail crosses North Fork Long Pine Creek and shortly enters the John Muir Wilderness, beyond the junction with the abandoned foot-trail section. Soon the forest cover thins, and the slope is covered with a chaparral that includes mountain mahogany, Sierra chinquapin and sagebrush. This steep slope can get very hot in midmorning, and the trip is best begun as early as possible. Breather stops on this trail section provide a "Veed" view down the canyon framing the Alabama Hills.

Then the trail levels off somewhat through several willow-covered pockets having a moderate forest cover of lodgepole and foxtail pines, and passes fields of corn lilies, delphinium, tall lupine and swamp whiteheads. In 1½ miles we approach a ford of Lone Pine Creek, which will be your first water source in late season. Beyond the log ford is a junction with a spur trail to nearby, visible Lone Pine Lake. We turn up a barren wash, then switchback up another rocky slope under a moderate lodgepole cover to Outpost Camp (called "Bighorn Park" on the topo map), a willow-covered meadow that was once a lake. Packers once used this meadow as the last grazing area on the ascent to the Sierra crest, and a packer's wife ran an overnight camp where food and tent-lodging could be bought.

Our trail veers away from the waterfall that tumbles down into Outpost Camp from the southwest, fords Lone Pine Creek and begins a short series of switchbacks beside the cascading creek, past blossoming creambush, Indian paintbrush, Sierra chinquapin, mountain pride, currant, pennyroyal, fireweed and groundsel. Then the trail boulder-hops the creek and arrives at Mirror Lake (10640'), cradled in its cirque beneath the south face of Thor Peak. This cold lake has fair fishing for rainbow and brook, but camping is no longer allowed here. The Forest Service closed the lake to camping in 1972 after severe overuse had created a montane slum. Since then, the lakeshore has begun to recover, and after a great many years it may look something like it did when first discovered.

Leaving Mirror Lake, the trail ascends the south wall of the Mirror Lake cirque via switchbacks. At the top of the ascent the trail passes timberline, as a last foxtail pine and a broken, weathered, convoluted whitebark snag are seen, along with a few last willows. Soon Mt. Whitney comes into view, over Pinnacle Ridge. From here, the rocky trail ascends moderately alongside the gigantic boulders on the north side of the South Fork of Lone Pine Creek. In the cracks in the boulders the hiker will find ivesia, cinquefoil, creambush, currant and much gooseberry, and looking across the canyon he will see the cascading outlet of Consultation Lake. Beside a rock bridge that crosses the stream are specimens of the moisture-loving shooting star. After ascending over some poured concrete steps — which unfortunately detract from the wilderness feel of this country — the trail arrives at the last campsites before the crest — Trail Camp (12000′). Here beneath Wotan's Throne is also the last reliable water in late season. There are numerous level campsites, but no wood.

As the trail begins the one hundred or so switchbacks to Trail Crest (the name of the pass), Mt. Whitney is occluded by a sharp spire, and Mt. Russell, farther north, comes into view. This rocky, barren talus slope is not *entirely* barren, for one may see a dozen species of flowering plants, climaxed by the multiflowered, blue "sky pilot." The building of this trail section involved much blasting with dynamite, and the natural fracture planes of the granite are evident in the blasted slabs. Finally the 1700′ ascent from Trail Camp ends at Trail Crest (13714′), and the hiker suddenly has vistas of a great part of Sequoia National Park to the west, including the entire Great Western Divide. To the east, far below, are Consultation Lake and several smaller, unnamed lakes, lying close under the Whitney crest. These lakes may not be free of ice the whole summer. From Trail Crest the route descends for a short ½ mile to the junction with the John Muir Trail, which terminates atop Mt. Whitney (see Trail #1).

"The maintenance of biological and mental health requires that technological societies provide in some form the biological freedom enjoyed by our Paleolithic ancestors."
                                                      Rene Dubos

TRAIL #12

Crabtree Meadow to Rock Creek (24 miles)

This loop trip, partly cross country, tours the remote, grand high country in the southeast corner of the quadrangle.

In Upper Crabtree Meadow, about ½ mile south of the Crabtree Ranger Station, a trail of use ascends to Crabtree Lakes. First the route takes us along the south side of the meadow, then it ascends moderately through a lodgepole forest, on a slope above Crabtree Creek. At the first Crabtree Lake is a packer campsite, but in comparison to campsites on the Muir Trail it is little used. Our route ascends moderately over boulders to the largest Crabtree Lake, with a spectacular wall just south of it, culminating in Mt. Chamberlain. As we approach this lake the trail ends on granite slabs and we keep well to the north on these slabs. Beyond the lake, staying on the north side of the creek, sometimes a slight distance from it, we arrive at the uppermost lake in this watershed.

From this lake we can see an obvious saddle to the southeast, and we reach it via a short, steep scramble, over talus. From this cairned saddle, the view west of Mt. Kaweah and Kaweah Peaks Ridge is excellent, and we have closer views of Mt. McAdie, Mt. Newcomb, and the flat-topped Major General, as well as the lakes on our path of descent. The first lake, Lake 12125, is utterly hemmed in by granite, and has no campsites. Making our way down the drainage southeastward, we circle Sky Blue Lake on its east side. Camping is possible here in several level, grassy spots, but there is no wood until we reach the next basin down the stream. This rocky basin provides the viewpoint for seeing "The Miter" as a miter.

The high, jagged, fractured, cliffed granite formations in this country are a great attraction for climbers, and some of them can be climbed without expertise (see *Climbers*).

Where the canyon narrows and the descent steepens, the timber cover increases to moderate, and foxtail joins lodge-pole. Eventually we begin to see a trail on the west side of the creek, well used and sometimes blazed. This trail threads a small, wet meadow and then becomes indistinct as it nears the unnamed lake on Rock Creek a short distance off the *Mt. Whitney* map. There are excellent campsites on the northwest side of this lake. A trail up the tributary to the east leads, in less than a mile, to a junction with the Army Pass trail. This tributary descends from the Soldier Lakes (unnamed on the topo map, lying south of The Major General). Good camp-sites may be found on the east side of the lower lake.

Past the outlet, the trail descends steadily alongside the now-cascading stream. The dense green forest cover provides the shade that gooseberries prefer, and these thorny, edible plants are frequent in this trail section. After about 2 miles the trail fords Rock Creek in a meadow lush with many species of wildflowers in mid season, and in another ¾ mile we meet and step onto the Pacific Crest Trail. This trail descends moderately through often-heavy lodgepole forest cover to the banks of Rock Creek, and soon reaches some large campsites.

Then, fording Rock Creek on a downed lodgepole, our

route veers north and climbs steeply up the canyon wall. The grade lessens as we ford Guyot Creek (last water for over 4 miles) and then increases again as we climb around boulders to a forested saddle. From this saddle there is an excellent view of Red Spur, a nearly barren hulk of reddish rock, on whose lake-dotted slopes one can spend days without seeing anybody. Then our route descends moderately to the large sandy basin of Guyot Flat. Geologists estimate that the sand here is over 100′ deep, and the resulting drainage affords little opportunity for plant seeding or growth.

Beyond Guyot Flat the trail undulates under a moderate forest cover before dropping steeply into the Whitney Creek drainage. On this descent we have views eastward of Mt. Whitney, looking most unlike its aspect from Lone Pine: it is broad, flat-topped, domish, and avalanche-chuted. Shortly before we reach Whitney Creek a trail of use goes west down the canyon, to the Kern River trail. At the creek ford is a good campsite, with good views and some wood. Up the creek 100 yards is another good campsite, and farther on a packer campsite. From the trail junction in Upper Crabtree Meadow where this loop began, it is only a short ascent to the John Muir Trail near the Crabtree Ranger Station.

Travel

THERE ARE THREE METHODS USED to travel the trails described in this book. They are 1) on foot, either by daywalks or with a backpack; 2) on horseback, with or without a pack string; or 3) on foot while leading a burro or a mule. Motorized vehicles are outlawed in Wilderness Areas and on trails in National Parks. The method one decides upon should take into account the purpose of the trip (fishing, nature study, photography, cross-country walking, etc.), grazing restrictions, personal condition (health, age), and length of time one plans to spend in the back country.

The most popular of the three is to go on foot with a backpack. The reasons given for this choice by backpackers is that they feel that backpacking lets one get "closer to the country," and that backpacking is more economical. Travel on horseback is a second choice employed by those who like the principle of long-term base camps, and/or those who are physically incapable of traveling long distances on foot. Those who lead burros or "walking mules" are, by definition, in-betweeners. (Note: availability of burros and "walking mules" should be determined with packers before deciding upon this method.)

"He who travels alone arrives alone."
                                        Lawrence Ferlinghetti

Backpackers

BECAUSE THE BACK-packer carries "his home on his back," he is free, within the limitations of stamina and food, to go as far as he likes. Two-week back-country trips are not overly long excursions if the backpacker plans his food and gear carefully. With caches or base-camp setups, he can extend his trip even longer. This prolonged duration is less a result of hardier backpackers being bred than of more and better light-weight equipment being manufactured.

Ever aware of the advantages of lightweight equipment and the increasing array of freeze-dried foods, the backpacker devotes his on-the-trail gab sessions to "shop talk." There is, in fact, a tendency to make a fetish of equipment, and "go-lighters" should constantly remind themselves of their purpose in going to wilderness. With this thought in mind, the editors have prepared the following list — an itemization of basics without a lengthy discussion of comparative differences in style.

Necessary

pack	line
bedroll	toilet paper
extra socks	waterproof matches
cooking pot(s)	warm jacket
spoon	knife
maps	soap
compass	raingear
flashlight	bandana
first aid kit	plastic bags
ground sheet	boots
plastic tarp	Sierra cup

Optional

foam pad/air mattress
stove
fuel container
canteen
tent
hat
insect repellent
toothbrush and paste
lip salve
sun-tan lotion
dark glasses
climbing rope

hiking shorts
paper towels
fork
prescriptions
extra clothing
notebook and pencil
ice axe
crampons
salt/pepper shaker
bowl
cooking pots
gloves

Luxury

mirror
wire grill
fishing gear
fishing license
air pillow
camp shoes
wrist watch
camera
binoculars

pot grippers
harmonica
recorder
guitar
sewing kit
wash basin
books
small towel

"The way to travel the farthest in the shortest distance,
is to go afoot."
                                        Henry David Thoreau

Packers

THOSE WHO PROVIDE RENTAL stock and guides for back-country trips into the Sierra are called "packers." Packers do not make a practice of outfitting their customers beyond the requisite stock, saddles and gearbags. Their usual service includes guiding, and the customer has the alternatives of having the stock and the wrangler/guide along for the duration of the trip, or asking for a "spot trip." The latter is an agreement between packer and guests that they and their gear will be transported to a designated campsite, and that the packer will return at a stipulated time to transport them back to the pack station.

Reservation arrangements for a packer's services should be made well in advance, and should include the following information in the initial correspondence:

1. How many persons will there be in your party?

2. Approximately what dates will you want to pack in and pack out?

3. To what lakes or to what area do you wish to pack?

4. If you have a route preference (perhaps described in this book) what is it?

5. Will you want the continuous hire of the packers and animals, or will you want a spot trip?

6. How many pounds do you estimate your pack load will be?

Prices for packers' services vary, and should be determined by correspondence with the individual packer.

Whether planning a trip on horseback or afoot, the basic clothing to be worn on the trail is the same. One should wear a long-sleeved shirt, durable trousers, light-weight inner socks (usually cotton), heavy outer socks (usually wool), and boots (riding boots/vibram-soled hiking boots). The following should be carried on one's person: knife, map, compass, matches, rubber bands, pencil, bandana, identification, Sierra cup.

Climbers

GOOD CLIMBING OPPORTUNIties are plentiful in the *Mt. Whitney* quad. There are 25 named peaks above 13,500 feet, and they all have impressive views, as do many of the lower peaks. Climbs are rated by their difficulty, beginning with class 1 and going through class 5. Class 1 routes are "walk ups" and class 2 routes are easy scrambles. An unusually large proportion of the peaks in *Mt. Whitney* are either class 1 or class 2, and thus are accessible to the average backpacker.

The following peaks have either class 1 or class 2 routes. (For details, see *Climbers Guide*, listed in the Bibliography.)

Mt. Barnard
Mt. Brewer
Mt. Bradley
Caltech Peak
Mt. Carillon
Center Peak
Mt. Chamberlain
Discovery Pinnacle
Mt. Ericsson
Mt. Genevra
Gregory's Monument
Mt. Guyot
Mt. Hale
Mt. Hitchcock
Mt. Irvine
Joe Devel Peak

Mt. Kawcah
Keeler Needle
Mt. Keith
Kern Point
The Major General
Mt. Mallory
Midway Mountain
Mt. Newcomb
Mt. Pickering
Picket Guard Peak
Red Spur
South Guard

Tawny Point
Thor Peak
Trojan Peak
Tunnabora Peak
Mt. Tyndall
University Peak
West Spur Peak
West Vidette
Mt. Whitney
Mt. Williamson
Wotan's Throne
Mt. Young

Peak 13540 (1 mil SW of Mt. Tyndall)
Peak 13030 (1 mi. S of Caltech Peak)
Peak 13285 (1.5 mi. NE of Mt. Kaweah)
Peak 13040+ (0.5 mi. E of Shepherd Pass)

STUDY TO BE QUIET

BIBLIOGRAPHY

Austin, Mary, *Land of Little Rain*, Doubleday, New York, 1961

Brewer, William H., *Up and Down California*, University of California Press, Berkeley, 1966

Brower, David., ed., *Wilderness Handbook*, Ballantine, New York, 1967

Farquhar, Francis, *History of the Sierra Nevada*, University of California Press, Berkeley, 1965

Ferber, Peggy, ed., *Mountaineering, the Freedom of the Hills*, The Mountaineers, Seattle, 3rd edition, 1974

Gudde, Edwin G., *California Place Names*, University of California Press, Berkeley, 1969

King, Clarence, *Mountaineering in the Sierra Nevada*, University of Nebraska Press, Lincoln, 1971

McDermand, Charles, *Waters of the Golden Trout Country*, G. P. Putnam's Sons, New York, 1946 (out of print)

Munz, Philip, *California Mountain Wildflowers*, University of California Press, Berkeley, 1963

Murie, Olaus, *Field Guide to Animal Tracks*, Houghton, Boston, 1958

Parsons, Mary, *Wildflowers of California*, Dover Publications, New York, 1966

Peters, Ed, ed., *Mountaineering, the Freedom of the Hills*, The Mountaineers, Seattle, 4th edition, 1982

Peterson, Roger, *A Field Guide to Western Birds*, Houghton Mifflin, Boston, 1961

Roper, Steve, *Climbers Guide to the High Sierra,* Sierra
     Club, San Francisco, 1976

Roth, Hall, *Pathway in the Sky,* Howell-North, Berkeley,
     1965 (out of print)

Sierra Club, *Sierra Club Bulletins* (various volumes), Sierra
     Club, San Francisco

Storer, Tracy, and Usinger, Robert, *Sierra Nevada Natural
     History,* University of California Press, Berkeley, 1963

Sudworth, George, *Forest Trees of the Pacific Slope,* Dover
     Publications, New York, 1967

OTHER WILDERNESS PRESS PUBLICATIONS

Schaffer, Jeffrey P. *et al., The Pacific Crest Trail, Vol. 1,*
     revised 1988

Weeden, Norman, *A Sierra Nevada Flora,* revised 1986

Winnett, Thomas, *The John Muir Trail,* revised 1984

Winnett, Thomas, *Backpacking Basics,* 1979

Winnett, Thomas and Jason Winnett, *Sierra South,* revised
     1986

OTHER WILDERNESS PRESS HIGH SIERRA HIKING GUIDES

Mineral King   *Triple Divide Peak*

Trail Profiles

The trail profiles on the following pages will help the hiker in his planning. With a pack of about 1/5 your body weight, you can expect to cover two horizontal miles per hour. Add one hour for each 1000 feet of elevation gain. Thus, if you are going 12 miles, and the total of all the "ups" is 1500 feet, you can expect to be walking for about: 6 hours + 1.5 hours = 7½ hours. This includes "normal" rest stops.

For downhill walking, use the figure of two miles per hour except where the trail is steep. A steep section will require an extra hour for 2000 feet of descent.

If you are walking without a pack, or you are in really excellent condition, you can do better — perhaps up to 50% better.

If you are walking cross country, it may take you all day to go even two miles. There is wide variation, depending on the slope, the footing, the ground cover, and your condition.

The symbol $\int$ means "ford," but there may be no running water there in the late summer. Since bridges require no fording, they are not shown.

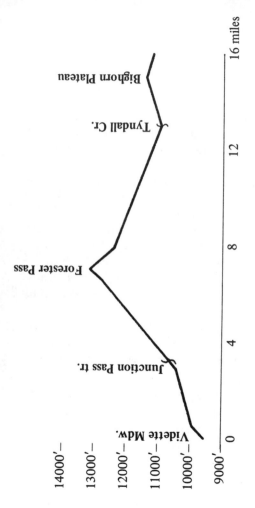

Vidette Mdw.
Junction Pass tr.
Forester Pass
Tyndall Cr.
Bighorn Plateau

14000'
13000'
12000'
11000'
10000'
9000'

0   4   8   12   16 miles

Trail #1

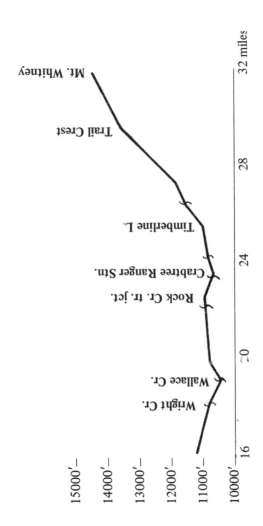

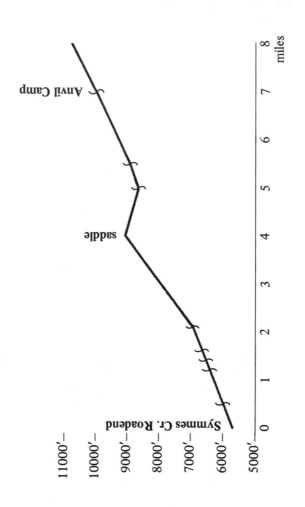

Trail #2

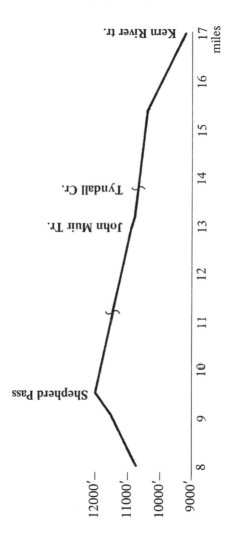

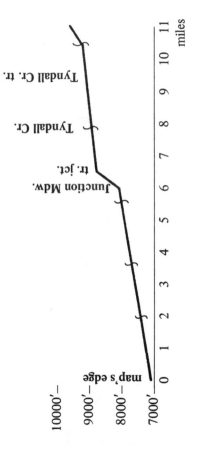

Trail #3

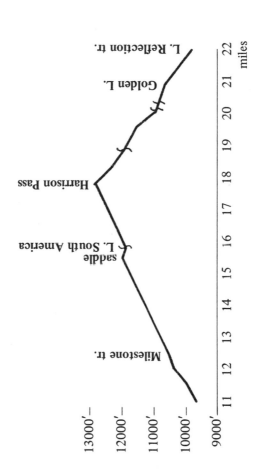

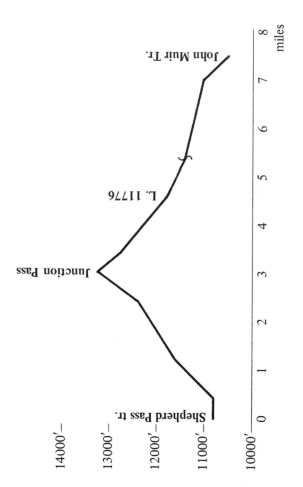

Trail #4

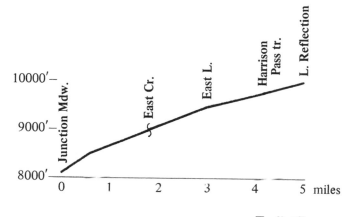

Trail #5

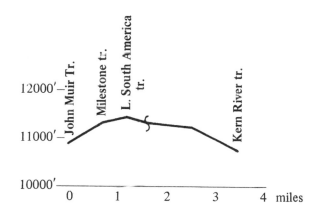

Trail #6

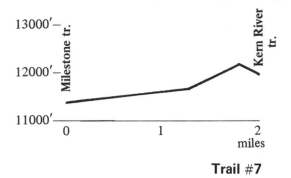

Trail #7

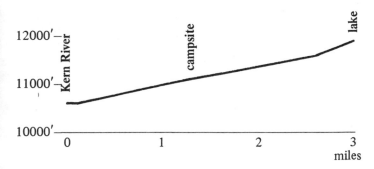

Trail #8

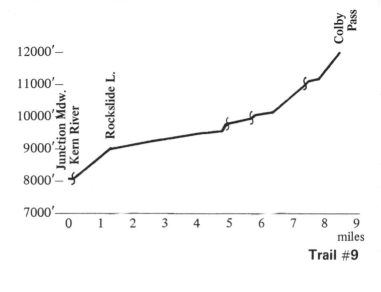

Trail #9

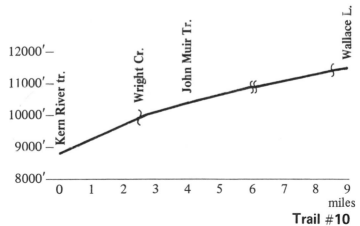

Trail #10

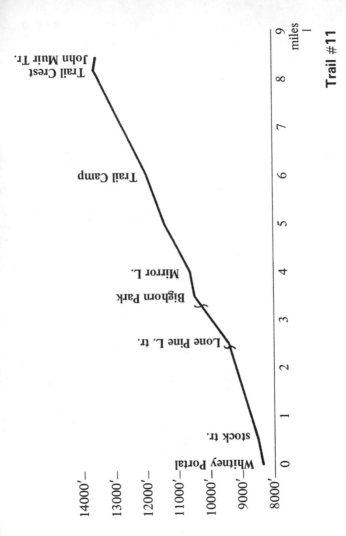

Trail #11

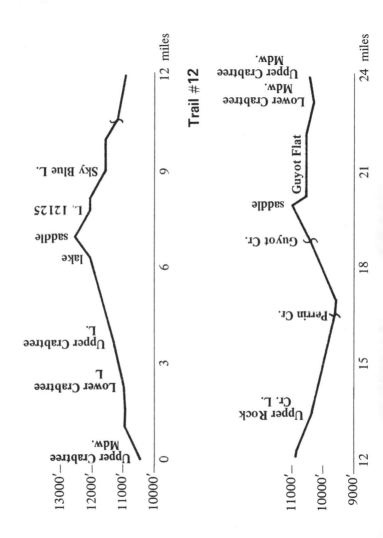

Trail #12

Index

Locating trails on the map

This list is included to help you locate trails on the book's map. Below is a list of the book's hikes, each one followed by a letter-number combination. Each combination refers to the grid section on the map that has the *start* of a route.

Trail No. 1: B1   Trail No. 7: C3
Trail No. 2: E1   Trail No. 8: B3
Trail No. 3: B5   Trail No. 9: B4
Trail No. 4: D2   Trail No. 10: B4
Trail No. 5: B1   Trail No. 11: E4
Trail No. 6: C3   Trail No. 12: C4